M000207547

CEREMONY FOR THE CHOKING GHOST

To Jennifer— I'm so glad to know you and share work with you. I hope we have many more years to hear one another.
Karen 2010

BY KAREN FINNEYFROCK

A Write Bloody Book
Long Beach. CA USA

Ceremony for the Choking Ghost
by Karen Finneyfrock

Write Bloody Publishing ©2010.
1st printing.
Printed in USA

Ceremony for the Choking Ghost Copyright 2010.
All Rights Reserved.

Published by Write Bloody Publishing.

Printed in Long Beach, CA USA.

No part of this book may be used or performed without written consent from the author, if living, except for critical articles or reviews.

Cover Designed by Joshua Grieve
Cover Art by Amanda Atkins
Interior Layout by Lea C. Deschenes
Edited by Derrick Brown, shea M gauer, Saadia Byram, Michael Sarnowski
Proofread by Sarah Kay
Interior Art by Brandon Lyon
Author Photo by Inti St. Clair
Type set in Helvetica Neue and Bell MT

To contact the author, send an email to writebloody@gmail.com

WRITE BLOODY PUBLISHING
LONG BEACH, CA

2

3

CEREMONY FOR THE CHOKING GHOST

This book is dedicated to organ donors.

BACK AROUND

Spring
cut palm fronds
and snuck them
up my skirt while I was sleeping.
Now my dress makes shushing noises
when I walk. The hem creeps from knee
to handful of thigh and hangs there,
a cotton lip, green fingers of the leaf
pointing down. Do your worst.

I'm not afraid of your clicking teeth
on the sidewalk. I know spring is hard
to keep quiet. I have melted ice into my
wrist to keep from talking to the wrong
kind of men, pants rolled to mid-calves,
feet slid into sandals like leather-tongue
dragons. Street vendors sell pickles.
I eat them wearing sunglasses.
These days, my body is always
a carousel animal. I'll be the
flamingo. You,
the horse.

PART ONE

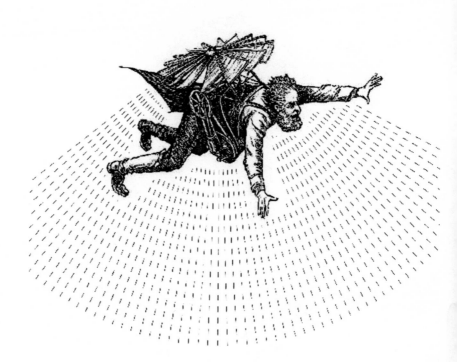

WHAT LOT'S WIFE WOULD HAVE SAID (IF SHE WASN'T A PILLAR OF SALT)

Do you remember when we met
in Gomorrah? When you were still beardless,
and I would oil my hair in the lamp light before seeing
you, when we were young, and blushed with youth
like bruised fruit. Did we care then
what our neighbors did
in the dark?

When our first daughter was born
on the River Jordan, when our second
cracked her pink head from my body
like a promise, did we worry
what our friends might be
doing with their tongues?

What new crevices they found
to lick love into or strange flesh
to push pleasure from, when we
called them Sodomites then,
all we meant by it
was neighbor.

When the angels told us to run
from the city, I went with you,
but even the angels knew

15

that women always look back.
Let me describe for you, Lot,
what your city looked like burning
since you never turned around to see it.

Sulfur ran its sticky fingers over the skin
of our countrymen. It smelled like burning hair
and rancid eggs. I watched as our friends pulled
chunks of brimstone from their faces. Is any form
of loving *this* indecent?

Cover your eyes tight,
husband, until you see stars, convince
yourself you are looking at Heaven.

Because any man weak enough to hide his eyes while his
      neighbors
are punished for the way they love deserves a vengeful god.

I would say these things to you now, Lot,
but an ocean has dried itself on my tongue.
So instead I will stand here, while my body blows itself
grain by grain back over the Land of Canaan.
I will stand here
and I will watch you
run.

GALACTIC CANNIBALISM

Scientists say that galaxies, those spiral windings
that turn on themselves (the legs of pole dancers,
the arms of Sufis), eventually bump into one another
in space, a clumsy polka, and finding each other, begin
to eat one another, like evenly matched cannibals
on a famished hunt; they start with the arms
and chew their way into deeper gravity.

Here is the danger of scientists and metaphor.

Galaxies do not sit in the black basement of space,
in the clock-less sleep of space, in the crow feather empty
of space waiting patiently for a meal. Their dance is less
polka, more tango, orbiting one another carefully,
a billion years of eye contact. Our own lonely Milky Way
has not known the touch of spiral arms since the big bang
erased all her home phone numbers.

Those great collections of dust when they touch, scientist,
are not devouring each other with their clumsy explosions
and sudden changes in gravity.

They are kissing
in the brief candlelight of their own suns.

17

THE BIRTHDAY PARTY

The year Beth was in the hospital,
Wayne didn't want Molly to turn three
listening to her mother's heart machine thump
like a goldfish with no bowl, so we took her to the
Baltimore aquarium. I spent the day brightening
my eyes when Molly looked at me. We saw manta rays.

We ate slices of Sicilian pizza in the food court and called it
birthday cake. I held the levee in my throat together with one hand
on my sweater. The other carried a girl through the shark
    tank, past
the phosphorous eyes of the cavefish, kicking and screaming
"Nemo!" at the clowns.

On Molly's third birthday, I prayed for a car accident
on the highway, a gang shooting that missed the chest.
Heart transplants are always a result of tragedy, old
and satisfied hearts won't work. In the dim hallway,
the blind jellyfish drift joblessly past, not on their
way anywhere. But to a swimmer, one careless
leg in a stormless summer, they always
seem vicious, sighted
intentional.

HOW TO IDENTIFY A DAMAGED GIRL

Eyeliner.

Straight line bruises below the eyelash. Gentle, mimic-shiners.
Bracelets. Zippers. Nervous look. Arms linked through the arms
of other damaged girls. Boots with soles thick as oil spills. Knees
that lean together like drunks at a picnic.

Their clothes are painted on. THEY YELL
WHEN YOU ARE NOT EXPECTING IT. Then they
      always cry.
Go ahead, tell them how unstable they are—
it makes them feel recognized. Tell them they bring it
on themselves—*that* makes them feel they have
control of something.

Damaged girls decorate their bodies like prisons at Christmas,
tinsel strung over the fleshy cages of their backs. Paper chains
of acrylic nails and fishnets. Cigarettes hang off their lips
like bridge jumpers who changed their minds. They find
the softest parts of themselves, pierce them.

Do you withhold your attention, knowing
they need it more than sleep? Do you hate the way
they make hand puppets of your lust? Do you want to rip
out their pink hearts like artichokes? You know they want

you to. It confirms their belief that lovers are violent. As they leak
artichoke blood all over the sidewalk, they sputter, "I knew it."

Her tattoos trap your eye in the rat-maze of her skin. This
broken doll in the accident median. You rubberneck
for the girl who owned her. The cotton-thread,
daisy-headed girl. That necessary, shining child.

MY JOB

In the lawn chair, bare toes—
the earthworm grass, crushed cans of Olympia
dandelion around me, three mosquito bites from a
personal record, re-checking the placement of Mars,
plastic cross hatches branding my bread thighs.

Electra has already slipped into the neck of Scorpio.
The dogs are loose. Orion doesn't come to Cassiopeia,
but she waits. Another pop top lets loose its hiss and
spit. I was born for this.

THE NEWER COLOSSUS

My feet have been wilting in this salt-crusted cement since
    the French sent me over
on a steamer in pieces. I am the new Colossus, wonder of
    the modern world,
a woman standing watch at the gate of power.

The first night I stood here, looking out over the Atlantic
    like a marooned sailor,
plaster fell from my lips parting and I said, "Give me your
    tired, your poor," like a
woman would say it, full of trembling mercy, while the rats
    ran over my sandals and
up my stairwell. I was young then, and hopeful.

I didn't know how Europe and Asia, eventually the Middle
    East, would keep pushing
their wretched through the bay like a high tide. I am
    choking on the words I said
about the huddled masses. They huddle on rafts leaving
    Cuba and we turn them
back. In sweltering truck backs crossing the desert, we
    arrest them. I heard about
a container ship where three Chinese hopefuls died from
    lack of oxygen pretending
to be dishrags for our dollar stores. How can we not have
    room for them? We still
have room for golf courses.

We still put swimming pools in our backyards and drive
    around with our back seats
empty. I am America's first liar, forget about George
    Washington. My hypocrisy
makes me want to plant my dead face in the waves. The
    ocean reeks of fish and
tourism. My optimist heart corrodes in the salt wind.

Give me your merchandise, I should say. Give me your
    coffee beans. Give me your
bananas and avocados, give me your rice. We turn our
    farmland into strip malls, give
me things to sell at my strip malls. Give me your ethnic
    cuisine, your cheaply-made
plastics, give me, by trembling boatload, your Japanese
    cars. Give me your oil.
Not so I can light my lamp with it, but to drool it from the
    thirsty lips of my lawn
mowers. Give me your jealousy, your yearning to crawl
    inside my hollow bones
and sleep in my skin made of copper. Look,

over there is New York. Doesn't it glow like the cherry
    end of a cigarette? Like a
nebula from the blackness of space out here in the harbor?
    Wait with me. Watch it
pulse like a hungry lion until morning. I should tell you to
    enjoy it from here. You
will never be allowed to come in.

JOSH'S FAVORITE TREE

Josh's favorite tree
is a western red cedar.
It's the way the boughs reach
out to scoop things off the ground,
especially boys whose toes grip the bark
like crows do telephone lines. Josh has turned
trees into afternoons and patio chairs, into
chalkboards and tight ropes. He even
made a tree into a telephone booth
once, but he never knew if the
call went through. He was
dialing the city of the dead,
where trees grow
upside down and
the branches look
like feet instead
of hands, and no one
owns time, and the crows don't have
telephone wires to sit on. They sit on
the ground. They look up
whenever they hear
the trees
ringing.

THE SECRET DISCIPLINE
for Tara, Danny, and Matt

The first word of this poem is *Death*.
It has been taken from the creation myth of my people
in which a turtle gives birth to a pregnant ocean.
In the story, the turtle is called *hurricane* and the ocean is called
the great salt lick of the water cow. I know because I am
my people's story keeper.

As a child I sat at the foot of aunts while dough fell
from their rolling pins and they spoke in the riddles
of hair curlers and gentlemen callers.

Caught listening and eating scraps, I was inaugurated
to the secret discipline and given paper as well as a washing
machine to sit on while dinner was being made.
This is where my people come from—

In Maryland, there is a lake so overrun with ducks
that duck poop has poisoned the fish and made the lake toxic.

Loan me your fingers to hold up the moon.
I am trying to read what I wrote on my paper knees.

In my town there is an army base that makes biological
weapons. Every summer they hold a carnival. Every evening
my grandfather would go to the root cellar and gather potatoes.

The aunts were the size of giants. They were always making dinner. My sister's heart failed. My cousin hit my grandfather in the head with a brick. When the people of my town die, they are taken into the arms of the Sky Pitcher.

I am my people's storyteller, I keep secrets with one set of my lips. This is the story of my people—

We hold death inside of us like jacks-in-the-box, we hold death like gifts we are waiting to give to our children, we are only alive long enough to take thirty thousand steps.

In our root cellar there are enough potatoes to built a pyramid to my ancestors. I come from the people of the toxic duck lake. I am the secret keeper of the washing machine. I sleep in the arms of the salt lick and the hurricane. My sister is with the Sky Pitcher. The ocean is made of a million arms. God lives in the way light reflects off of water.

WAKE

When your eyes have dripped down to your chin,
and your mouth is a window in summer, bangs swept
to the side of the nose on your tilted windmill face, I will
still think you look like a broken clock, stopped on the morning
we hid under the covers while the phone rang and the teakettle
screamed to murder sleep, pillow giggling in the dust ruffle
where morning couldn't get at us.

Remember how strong the dollar was then?

DOCTORS

He scans my family history, a quick supermarket cashier,
red laser pausing on his bar code fingers. *"Thirty-six?"*
he asks, surprised by the price of apples.
The Earth pretends to be a girl.
"Heart failure?" he says, and satellites fall out of the sky.
My eyes are dark computer monitors. Another
electrical storm.
"Did her doctors know why?" Eclipse.
"Virus maybe, possibly a congenital family trait,"
I answer, even get to the part where I say *"it may have been
a result of the pregnancy,"* before dirt blows out of my
mouth instead of words. Shoulder shrug. Dust bowl.
Now the nurse, eyes like melting snow asks,
"Did she carry the baby to term?"
In the earthquake, my head
shakes and shakes and shakes.

PART TWO

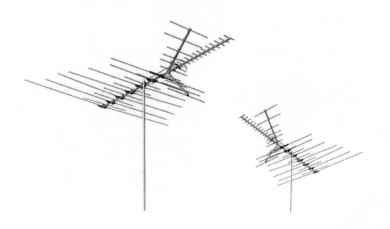

THE RUBE GOLDBERG MACHINE

Our last names were close enough in the alphabet to be
    tongue kissing, so we ended
up lab partners in physics class. That's why we built the machine.

I was a freshman, never kissed by a boy, call me "late to
    bloom." He was
a junior, lanky even for the track team, call him a
    "reluctant virgin." And a Rube
Goldberg Machine is a complex device that performs a
    simple task, like a pendulum
knocking open a trap door that drops a hammer, all for the
    purpose of pounding
a nail. It was forty-five percent of our grade.

Teenagers make out in forgotten places: parking lots past
    closing time,
city parks after dark. We went to my basement, my
    parent's footsteps
whispering over the ceiling like gossip.

It started with a cue ball rolling down a hamster chute,
    then knocking
over a candle onto a book, setting it ablaze. It was a commentary
on book burning. (We were very alternative.)

We learned a lot down there. Did you know that if you
        have long hair and
take off your sweater in a dark room, static stars erupt like
        Fourth of July
sparklers? Did you know that friction is the heat produced
        by teenagers
rubbing their blue jeans together? Science is a tricky
        fascination.

The candle kept snuffing out before the book could catch
        fire. He said, "We
need gasoline."

I was a good girl, barely comfortable with second base. I
        did not bring
combustible liquids to school.

So every night we tried something new: a shorter candle, a
        longer wick. "Gasoline,"
he said, unhooking my bra like a combination locker. "No,"
        I said, sucking his tongue
like a frozen flagpole. "Gasoline," he said, thumbing my
        nipples like Play Station
controllers. "No," I said, reaching into his pants like a
        beehive. "Gasoline!" he
said, pulling off my underwear like he was a magician and
        my panties were a
tablecloth . . . *Tada!*

Our project was due the next day and was still not
    reaching a satisfactory
conclusion. In exasperation, we soaked the book in
    kerosene and lit up
our science class like the encore at a Bon Jovi concert.

In the end, we made third base more times than the girl's
    softball team. We both
got A's in physics and my mom found my panties behind
    the dryer but she didn't
press me about it. Then he left me for my best friend,
    whom he eventually
married, and no one got their heart broken, except for me
    a little bit. I learned
more about science than I could have gotten out of any
    textbook. Especially one
that had never been set on fire.

NIGHT THINGS
for Michael and Kendra

Remember the night we walked through the cornfield
in late October with only the purpose of getting
lost, and the monstrous, dead sunflowers hung
their exhausted heads over us, spitting seeds
onto our shirts like they were handing us their babies.
I'm sure they pulled their knotty feet from the teeth of the earth
to follow us through the maze of dying things, but I
    couldn't catch them
moving. You and Kendra tossed used nitrous canisters into
    your backpacks
until they rattled like ghost chains as you laughed and
    swerved down the
hedgerows while I walked darkly behind you, muttering
    into the tall corn,
In Xanadu did Kubla Khan/ A stately pleasure-dome decree, because
the scene was gothic and the line stuck in my head so I knew how
the sunflowers felt with all those seeds crammed in their faces,
and the ground was half-flooded, black Washington state mud
searching fruitlessly for holes in our boots but managing
to lick our jeans to the knees, our fingers numb where
they grew from our gloves and you and Kendra, holding
hands all the way through the labyrinth, except when
you didn't, deciding to get lost apart, daring anything to
    scare you,

35

kick fighting back at the corn stalks when they got too
    menacing, declaring
yourselves and becoming the most frightening night
    things of Autumn.

VENUS FLY TRAP

You told me a relationship could cure
your loneliness. We wouldn't last through
the winter. My chest was a medicine cabinet,
you had insomnia, so you ate my liver.
This is how I helped you sleep.

Due to the incision, I leave drops of blood behind me
like bread crumbs. This is how you can find me again.

My body is a clock ticking in the belly of an alligator.
Your body is a sugar cube on a racehorse's tongue.
This is how our sexes love each other.

My body is a snapdragon, a Venus
fly trap, I can't help it.

Your body is an arrow out of the quiver. My body, a bow.

If your body is a boat, am I the lake, or the fish swimming
there? I look up at your wooden, salt-bleached self.
I push my fin, my waves, whatever moves me. This is how
    I help you go.

HER BODY BECOMES A HOSPITAL

In the first operation, they took the baby.
In the second, her heart's work was outsourced
to a machine the size of a suitcase. They told us we could
take her home, but first

we had to learn how to change the batteries, operate
the pump manually in case of power outage.
That summer Katrina turned storms into boogeymen,
the closets of the eastern seaboard were full of them.

When he was little, my uncle had polio. At the end of his
tiny life, the hospital breathed for him. One night a storm
dragged its potential fingers across Ohio, pulling the plug
from the socket of the Midwest. The hospital shut its eyes.
It looked like it was praying, but maybe it was just counting
to ten. Nurses called my grandfather to come and pump
    the iron lung.
All night, Harold Freeman was John Henry and death was
    the train.

My father paid electricians to fix the wires between
our house and the grid. I practiced in darkness,
the heatless quiet, with my feet, my elbows
and hands, repeating one motion for hours,
praying I could do it, force bellows to beat,
force iron to breathe.

ELEPHANT TOWN

Two towns over and a hundred miles from here, elephants
    are building a city.

They haven't mastered hammers, but are good at felling
    trees. They use their
trunks to raise barns together. In the heat of one
    afternoon, twelve elephants
can erect two houses with elephant-sized beds and big,
    elephant doorways.
They don't need bathrooms. The elephants still bathe in
    the current
of the Columbia, trumpeting river water over their
    rapturous hides.

No human has seen them building. They refuse to let us
    close enough to watch.
But once, three kids huddled in the watery pool of their
    streetlights. They saw two
elephants position a cupola on top of Elephant Town Hall,
    their mouths gaping
and necks straining with the weight. Their trunks held the
    massive pagoda while
elephant engineers prepared the architecture. The kids
    said the trunks looked
like rubbery telescopes. That the elephants appeared to be
    searching for
something in the sky.

CRYSTAL RADIO

When electrical lines first snaked their way through the
    rural South, the people
flipped on their light switches and said, *Look, now we have
    power.*

Then they formed a half-moon around the bare-bulb, and
    staring, wondered
at its mysteries.

    Light bulbs work like this:
    a filament, bent in two like a politician's tongue,
        and fitted into a fragile
    glass bird's egg of a bulb, is heated by a current of
        electricity
    traveling through wires hidden behind the walls.

    If this sounds hard to believe, consider for a
        moment the diamond.

    Diamonds were once the lumps of coal slipped into
        Christmas
    stockings of bad primordial children. Diamond
        mines worked by
    slaves in Africa grew up as coalmines worked by
        poor men in West

Virginia. The diamond trade funds world
        terrorism, flowing in a river
of ring fingers un-marshaled by the banks.

Diamonds are made of carbon under pressure. Oil
        is made of carbon
under pressure. You are made of carbon. Are you
        decomposing or
retaining your composure? Do your atoms
        rearrange themselves when
you aren't looking? Do you look in the mirror and
        see a donkey or an
elephant looking back; are you becoming a political party?

Do your thoughts look like light bulbs, and if so,
        what electricity is heating
them? What fuels your belief system? Is your brain
        a coalmine?
What do you dig for in there with your pick axe?
        Does the canary still sing
in your mind or is it suffocating? Do you worry at
        night that you might be a
slave in someone else's diamond trade? Have you
        ever had a cave-in
from blasting unwisely, tell me?

If your brain is a coalmine, is your heart then a
        nuclear reactor? Has your
heart ever split like an atom? What did it do to the
        rest of the cells of your

41

body? Could your heart cause a chain reaction? Can
    it make enough
energy to light up the cities in your organs? Could
    it make enough energy
to light up the cities in my organs? Are we
    connected on an electrical grid?

Who is monitoring our transmissions, deciding
    where the power lines go
to? Are they controlling our blackouts? Are they
    selling the energy of our
hearts and minds back to us? Do we let them?

When electrical lines first snaked their way through the
    rural South, the people
flipped on their light switches, formed a half-moon around
    the bare bulb, and said
the wrong thing.

They should have said, *This is nothing new. We have always
    glowed like that.*

It was never the electric companies that gave us power.

MISS YOU

After the affair, we didn't speak for two months.
When we saw each other again, he hugged me and
    whispered in my ear, "Miss you."
Too stingy to include the I.

   Miss you.   Like he was a fragment in search of a pronoun.
   Miss U!   Or he was at a football game rooting for
   Mississippi State.
   Miss You I have just won a beauty pageant in the
   State of Myself.

So I push him away and say, "That's *Ms. Me* to you."
No I don't.

He says "Miss you" and my heart goes carousel and
    jackhammer, because he
misses me—or, ostensibly, *he* is the one missing me, at least *someone*
or possibly *something* misses me and it feels good, the way
    cold chicken tastes
like steak when you're starving.

So, I ask myself, what is the least I would settle for? What
    if he just said "Miss…"
and looked at me pointedly? What if he just pushed out the
    "Meh." Could I scrape

together the missing letters until he missed me in three
    phantom syllables,
the ghost of my desire to be longed for?

After he leaves, I pull the words from my ear, fold them,
    put them
in my purse. I might be hungry later.

RICHARD BRAUTIGAN

Bobbie said it couldn't be counted as suicide,
not really.

That a drunk, in some ways, is already dead.

But that a drunk who keeps firearms
around the house,
shoots them off after midnight at the rabbits
in the back lot, at the rust eating the door hinge,
will eventually blow his brains out
from boredom.

I wanted to tell Bobbie that I knew you better than that.
But I never knew you.

I've known some drunks though.

A DETROIT TAROT

So the belly-dancing psychic says to me, one finger
    swirling toward the sky like an
errant lightning rod, "Here's the deal, I'm pretty drunk, so
    I can't give you a full Tarot
reading, but if you tell me your question, I'll pull a few cards."

She says this in her Detroit accent, so it sounds like she's
    negotiating knock-off time
for the union crew at the auto plant. We are still awake at
    the end of the party,
drinking wine from Yugoslavia out of a bottle shaped like
    a woman.

"My question," I say, holding the Tarot deck nervously like
    they are note cards for a
debate speech, "is about love."

She looks at me like I have just made a smart-ass joke
    about the Pistons and she
says, "Could you be a little more specific?"

"Like, will I find any soon?" I say, my voice growing
    twenty years younger in my
throat, my voice growing a mermaid tail and a unicorn horn.

Christina (whose name is spelled on her Tarot business
     card with an X like "Xtina")
lays down three cards, making the sound doctors make,
     "um hummm," she says,
"well, now I know who you are. You construct men out of
     paper and glue and attach
them to skies made of cardboard. You Mr. Potato them
     with the heads of high school
teachers and the hearts of Brontë characters. You wrap
     string around muscle
Voodoo dolls and hide them under your pillow…" and as
     dryly as I can muster it,
I say, "Go on."

Placing three more cards below the first, she says "Ah ha,
     ten of wands, three of
cups, you daily trip over fishing lines, cut yourself on the
     pages of mystery novels,
you're always burning the house down to build castles out
     of pillows. You need to tie
down the ropes of your dirigible, let the carnival wheels be
     still—there is one more
thing I have to tell you, come closer, let me whisper…you
     treat intimacy like
underwear, always hiding it under your skirt."

Xtina has turned my wine back into water, only now it
     contains salt. I'm about to say

47

"Best to let sleeping cards lie," when she draws three more
    and yells "I know, I know
what you need to do to find love!"

Christina, Cleopatra eyeliner and dark red lips, flowered
    headband and hoop
earrings, Detroit racing through her past like a V8 engine,
    is leaning toward me, her
breasts sitting in the cups of her bra like sleeping kittens,
    eyelids blinking too slow.
She says, "Karen, this is what the cards are telling me, this
    is how you will find love,"
her fingers pinched together like she could pull raindrops
    out of the sky, she says,
"when one of these men who turns you on is turning you
    on, tell him he is turning
you on."

I always thought that when a drunk, belly-dancing, Tarot-
    psychic met me at a party
and offered me the key to love like free tickets to a cabaret,
    I would wonder over its
metaphorical complexity. But I knew, that night, a wise
    woman had offered me
everything she gleaned from reading the stars in women's
    eyes. A powerful seer,
brought up by the daughters of the automakers.

48

PART THREE

THE MACHINE SPEAKS

Come lover and violate me with the ten cocks
of your hands. With the cock of your tongue,
with the cocks of your eyeballs and fists.
I am open as the night. Step in.

Before you, I had no reason to press
my chest against the kitchen table,
flattened-out back like a book spine.
Read backwards. Read me right to left.

Take your shovel hands, your trowel and rake
hands, turn my spine into a tree that drops sticky
fruit on my shoulders. Orchard my feet into rooting.
Bonsai my limbs an alphabet for birds. Look at me.
I am about to spill my loneliness all over your stomach.

Tell me our skin doesn't house spirits if you can bear
to push the lie past your teeth. Snap the bolts on my doors.
Refer to my body as your body. Find the clock spring, take
it out. Let me be your wind-up walking bird, still until you
touch my turn wheel. Look at me. Crank. Look at me.

HOW MY FAMILY GRIEVED

Many things are pointless.
    The word *unbearable*.

Other things have edges.
    I'll get Molly from school today.

We sandpapered down to the meaning of necessary things.
Among the condolence cards that jack-potted through
the mail slot daily was this one.

    I was so sorry to hear about Beth. I was also
    surprised to find out that Karen isn't married yet.

When humor gets too black, it turns into night.
The card had a sunset on the cover.

We twisted our hair into nets, watched
the bridges of each other's noses for jumpers.
The CIA could not have watched Molly more closely.

One day when I was alone with her, she said,
    Auntie, why are you crying?
Lying is one of the pointless things.
        I'm crying about your mommy.
    She doesn't want you to cry.

It's possible to sharpen the lead in a pencil
until the tip is so fine it becomes invisible.
It slices the air into particles as you lower it,
but as soon as it touches paper, it breaks.

Breaking is a pointless thing.

RODEO QUEEN MEETS ELEPHANT BOY

Waiting for you, I dipped my nails in house paint and shined
my belt buckles. Sprinkled glitter on my chaps and
    stirrups, I didn't want
you to miss me. I took the barrel races like a bull runner.
    My horse
became a motorbike. When I roped, I slid from the saddle
    like I was
dancing with the mare.

Before I knew you were coming, I made a map to the mud bank,
tripled the size of my doorframe.

You carry the desert dried in your circus knuckles. You
    smell like trunks
and bones. Your tail wants to be held again. The skin
    under your eyes
holds the weight of careless applause.

I saved the moments I waited for you in this jar.
Open it in front of me. Let me smell the air.

OH, CANADA

On a weekend in early summer I take the train to visit my
    lover in Canada.

Oh, Canada. Your cities are so European; Portuguese
    restaurants show World Cup
soccer on old televisions; but you are tied to America like a
    balloon to the wrist of a
young boy who keeps pulling the legs off of insects for pleasure.

Oh, America, you are spilling ice cream down your shirt again.

I have a lover in Canada, a musician whose heart is always
    on tour, but whose hands
are easy to love like the paws of a puppy, too big for
    navigating slippery surfaces.
I wrap back into his arms and forget the war in my
    country. It's Saturday morning,
my lover is sleeping, it's quiet.

And then…like the gradual song of an approaching ice-
    cream truck, she showed up.
All twenty-some years of her blushed onto her cheeks,
    she's from Switzerland and
has just flown in to Canada to surprise the musician she
    made love to on tour.

Oh, Switzerland, didn't anyone teach you not to surprise a
        man who makes
entrances and exits for a living?

There is nothing about my lover that implies fidelity. We
        are divining wands, he and
I, always leaning towards water. But when I look at her, so
        full of passport stamps
and Alpine run-off, a girl of chocolate and creamy mild
        cheese, I feel old and
ashamed of settling into this friendly sex.

Oh, Switzerland.

While in Canada, I met a woman of some Middle Eastern
        descent who told me,
If one more motherfucker asks me where I'm from, I'm going to
        fucking spit!
Some woman asked me where I'm from, I told her "my
        mother's cunt," she said,
"that's pretty crass," I said, "what's wrong, you never heard
        of Cuntistan?"

Oh, Cuntistan. Many a night have I spent in your humid
        valleys, a kiss of moist air
on my skin. I will not forget your full moons or fertile
        earth rank with the musk of
coming summer.

Oh, Switzerland, you are not Cuntistan. You are a little
    miss with the accent of
innocence. I hope he told you I was his sister.

In Canada, I visited a female friend and met her lover of
    fourteen years. When asked
how they kept it together, he said *I kept stepping aside for
    other men.* They counted
ten together on their fingers, then she said, *you'd better get
    going, my boyfriend will*
be here soon.

That night, I slept in my lover's room while he stayed up
    late with Switzerland.
Near dawn he woke me, rummaging around for a box of condoms.

Oh, Canada, I'm not Switzerland. I'm not Cuntistan either.
    I can't be your country
of safe houses or the last leg of your tour. You can't be my
    expatriate weekend, my
wrist-tied balloon. I have to go back to America, to raise
    the boy with books instead
of toy bullets. But as for you and Cuntistan, I could not
    forget the country
of my birth.

UNEASY HEAVENS AWAIT THOSE FLEEING

In the Golden Eternity tonight, they are button fixing.
    Turning rings around
hour-hand fingers, nail-biting their ghost thumbs to the
    skin. They consternate
in the milk-heavy clouds.

Nervous as lightning rods and eager, papers fall off desks,
    silent movie
projector house empty, only their watches keep beeping.
    They are swinging low,
three bobby pins from disheveled. Bathroom lights go on
    and then television sets,
they are bomb-scaring tonight, wearing the carpet to
    thread. They are chariots to
the golden horses pulling, hoping the sun will come soon.
    Clouds telescope,
rearrange themselves into arrows, choirs are learning the
    secret names for North,
practicing them *Holy, Holy,* coffee is brewing. Six sets of
    angel wings catch fire.
Heaven's women twist necklaces til they break. Hallways
    fold up like airplanes
made of tin. They re-check the blinds as cars gravel up the
    driveway, head-lighting
their way through cloud fog. *Have they come?*

Has the Golden Eternity savaged through the oyster gates
　　of the Kingdom?
Horsemen at their backs, mule carts of personal effects,
　　stomping dust
into dust, hands full of glaciers melting. Are their arms
　　still full of California?
Do they carry the child soldiers? Are the beds made? Will
　　there be enough milk
in the morning when the refugees have settled? Is that
　　them now?
The sound of four million feet scaring the silver cobbles.

Did you see the look in their eyes as they stumbled past
　　the wall of St. Peter?
Do they look like they are happy to be home?

THE RIGHT SCREWDRIVER

Half a heart is like half a vinyl record.

Half a heart is useful as half a shovel,
better than fingers if you're buried alive.

Half a heart works like half a highway;
it leaves you stranded.
Half a heart is like half an airplane—worse, like half a parachute.
Half a heart is half a guitar. I don't feel so good.

Did she think I could collect my artery wires,
a heap of fiber optics and copper, fix up
with the right screwdriver? My mother
always told me, *Be careful.*
Don't trust humans like robots.
Humans follow less loyal instincts.
Dismantle you for parts. Tell you what you lacked was passion.

Half a broken heart is like half a vinyl record.
I sit in my room and listen to the needle fall
onto the turntable and thud
and thud and thud.

THE BOAT HOUSE APARTMENTS

Tonight the couple in the next room makes love like radiators,
squealing and steaming into each other's mouths.
The man downstairs sleeps—an oil furnace.
Upstairs, the woman with the meaty ankles
shuffles her slippers over the floor, a wooden ship
aching its cold water. My vibrator acts like a furious
moth, beating itself against my clitoris as if I were a bug light.

The apartment building speaks to us, saying:
I appear to be made of quarry and fist, but I am days,
the nylon thread of nights. You look like people—all made
out of bodies—but you are really hours,
made up only of minutes.

You are gone quick as condensation evaporating off my
cement. Don't spend yourselves quietly.
You have this one night. Go ahead. Disturb the neighbors.

THE MAN ON TELEVISION

The man on the television
who just lost his wife and daughter
to some plane crash, house fire, car pile-up story is saying:
I don't hold animosity to the pilot, driver, God, the arsonist,
I know people have been through worse.

So, someone please (eyes in the camera) *tell me*
how to go on. You who have been through it,
tell me what to do next.

No one ever taught him how to hold a press conference.
All that honesty cradled between channels five and seven.
Hearing him was like seeing a seagull in the grocery store.

These are the only phone calls we should ever make.
Every e-mail should contain the subject line,
"What to do next."

Dear man on television,
please stay with us, our shifty faces
that are not hers, our bodies that brazenly
wear the same parts, our memories that approach
the outline of her and do not cross it.

Dear pigeon in the drugstore,
at night when grief turns your breath black,
and you breathe it alone among cereal boxes and medication,
resist breaking a wing on the windows. Every lock is made
with a key.

REBECCA AND HER LOVER ATE OYSTERS

Rebecca and her lover ate oysters.
They dressed in velvet, ordered wine before
appetizers, squirmed in their seats like jellyfish.

They were lesbians in love (eating oysters) in velvet over cocktails.

Waiters buzzed about their table like they were a field of lilies.
There was a lilac branch for a centerpiece, a votive candle
in the Mason jar and Rebecca's lover with androgynous hands
sliding muscles down her throat.

One oyster shell had a natural handle, cement crusting
where the knife pried it still breathing water from a rock.

Rebecca's flour-dry hand, ringed in glass and silver, reached
across the table for the oyster handle like a telephone receiver,
dialed her lover's number.

In velvet and cocktails she slid the body of the animal onto
      her tongue—
suspicious henchman of her throat—warning her against
      swallowing.
With olive juice fingers she reached between her conch shell lips
and pulled out one perfectly formed pearl.

In twenty-two years, the waiter had never seen one, brought
free bottles of wine, this really happened. This spot of sand
in an oyster's ovary became the polished tooth
of a mermaid. There were no storms at sea that night.

No one dropped his wallet in the street.
Circuits didn't short anywhere,
but everyone drank a little more than they should have.

Waiters danced around their table like they were a bonfire.
They held each other's gazes like engagement rings.
The other diners applauded and everyone offered to pay,
saying (but never loudly enough to be heard),
Here is enough reason, for one more day,
to keep vainly believing God loves us.

PART FOUR

LIKE YOU SAID IT WOULD

The kids at school claim fevers,
hand their laughs to spring, new
and generous, dropping its pollinated
water all over me, sweating pink
salt into my eyes. Go ahead,
spring, pee on my grass.

Let boys come to school without deodorant.
Let boiler rooms cook painted windows
into brick. Let me go to bed cozy and wake up freezing,
spring, do these things. Let men fill my boxes with mail.
Let them pineapple after me. Let them circle my building
in the evening humming throaty *come out of your house
tonight, Karen* songs. Let them offer beds of tulips, draw
close with toothbrushes tapping at my fire escape.
Let each pull a hair from his head and hold it
between his fingers. Let us see which one
the wind carries in.

THANK YOU

A shamefully incomplete list of people who made this possible:

Buddy Wakefield, Derrick Brown, Robbie Q. Telfer, Tara Hardy, Roger Bonair Agard, Roberto Ascalon, Matt Gano, Daemond Arrindell, Sara Brickman, Danny Sherrard, Ryler Dustin, Denise Jolly, Steven Wilbur, and Anis Mojgani.

Organizations that have supported and sustained me:

Richard Hugo House, Poetry Slam, Inc, Seattle Arts and Lectures, Youngstown Cultural Arts Center, Arts Corps, Hedgebrook.

I also thank my family for allowing me to share the story that belongs to all of us. For me, there is some healing.

ABOUT THE AUTHOR

Karen Finneyfrock is a poet, novelist, and teaching artist. A ten-year veteran of Poetry Slam stages, Karen was honored as a "Slam Legend" at the National Poetry Slam in Austin, Texas, and has performed her work at venues across North America. Her first book of young adult fiction, *Celia the Dark and Weird*, will be published by Viking Children's Books in 2011. Karen is a Writer-in-Residence at Richard Hugo House and teaches with Seattle Arts and Lectures' Writers in the Schools program. She lives in artist housing in a hundred-year-old school house with a red rug and drafty windows and real working lockers in the halls.

OTHER GREAT WRITE BLOODY BOOKS

EVERYTHING IS EVERYTHING (2010)
New poems by Cristin O'Keefe Aptowicz

DEAR FUTURE BOYFRIEND (2010)
A Write Bloody reissue of Cristin O'Keefe Aptowicz's first book of poetry

HOT TEEN SLUT (2010)
A Write Bloody reissue of Cristin O'Keefe Aptowicz's second book of poetry
about her time writing for porn

WORKING CLASS REPRESENT (2010)
A Write Bloody reissue of Cristin O'Keefe Aptowicz's third book of poetry

OH, TERRIBLE YOUTH (2010)
A Write Bloody reissue of Cristin O'Keefe Aptowicz's fourth book of poetry
about her terrible youth

THE BONES BELOW (2010)
New poems by Sierra DeMulder

CEREMONY FOR THE CHOKING GHOST (2010)
New poems by Karen Finneyfrock

MILES OF HALLELUJAH (2010)
New poems by Rob "Ratpack Slim" Sturma

RACING HUMMINGBIRDS (2010)
New poems by Jeanann Verlee

YOU BELONG EVERYWHERE (2010)
Road memoir and how-to guide for travelling artists

LEARN AND BURN (2010)
Anthology of poems for the classroom. Edited by Tim Stafford and Derrick Brown.

STEVE ABEE, GREAT BALLS OF FLOWERS (2009)
New poems by Steve Abee

SCANDALABRA (2009)
New poetry compilation by Derrick Brown

DON'T SMELL THE FLOSS (2009)
New Short Fiction Pieces By Matty Byloos

THE LAST TIME AS WE ARE (2009)
New poems by Taylor Mali

ANIMAL BALLISTICS (2009)
New poems by Sarah Morgan

CAST YOUR EYES LIKE RIVERSTONES INTO THE EXQUISITE DARK (2009)
New poems by Danny Sherrard

SPIKING THE SUCKER PUNCH (2009)
New poems by Robbie Q. Telfer

THE GOOD THINGS ABOUT AMERICA (2009)
An illustrated, un-cynical look at our American Landscape. Various authors.
Edited by Kevin Staniec and Derrick Brown

THE ELEPHANT ENGINE HIGH DIVE REVIVAL (2009)
Anthology

THE CONSTANT VELOCITY OF TRAINS (2008)
New poems by Lea C. Deschenes

HEAVY LEAD BIRDSONG (2008)
New poems by Ryler Dustin

UNCONTROLLED EXPERIMENTS IN FREEDOM (2008)
New poems by Brian Ellis

POLE DANCING TO GOSPEL HYMNS (2008)
Poems by Andrea Gibson

CITY OF INSOMNIA (2008)
New poems by Victor D. Infante

WHAT IT IS, WHAT IT IS (2008)
Graphic Art Prose Concept book by Maust of Cold War Kids and author Paul Maziar

IN SEARCH OF MIDNIGHT: THE MIKE MCGEE HANDBOOK OF AWESOME (2009)
New poems by Mike McGee

NO MORE POEMS ABOUT THE MOON (2008)
NON-Moon poems by Michael Roberts

JUNKYARD GHOST REVIVAL (2008)
with Andrea Gibson, Buddy Wakefield, Anis Mojgani, Derrick Brown, Robbie Q,
Sonya Renee and Cristin O'Keefe Aptowicz

…ND DESTROY (2008)
…eam up for a collection of non-sappy love poetry.

…007)
…dy & wild prose by Buzzy Enniss

…ING (2007)
…s by Buddy Wakefield

…ION SPARROWS ELECTRIC WHALE REVIVAL (2007)
…etry compilation by Buddy Wakefield, Anis Mojgani, Derrick Brown, Dan
Leamen & Mike McGee

I LOVE YOU IS BACK (2006)
Poetry compilation (2004-2006) by Derrick Brown

BORN IN THE YEAR OF THE BUTTERFLY KNIFE (2004)
Poetry anthology, 1994-2004 by Derrick Brown

SOME THEY CAN'T CONTAIN (2004)
Classic poetry compilation by Buddy Wakefield

WRITEBLOODY

WWW.WRITEBLOODY.COM